The Book of Parables

By Enoch

Copyright © 2019 Lamp of Trismegistus. All rights reserved. No part of this publication may be reproduced or transmitted in any form or by any means, electronic or mechanical, including photocopying, recording, or by any information storage and retrieval system, without permission in writing from Lamp of Trismegistus. Reviewers may quote brief passages.

ISBN: 978-1-63118-429-1

Christian Apocrypha Series

Other Books in this Series and Related Titles

The Lives of Adam and Eve by Moses
(978-1-63118-414-7)

The First and Second Gospels of the Infancy of Jesus Christ
by Thomas and James (978-1-63118-415-4)

Lost Chapters of the Book of Daniel and Related Writings by Daniel
(978-1-63118-417-8)

The Book of the Watchers by Enoch (978-1-63118-416-1)

The Smoky God or A Voyage to the Inner World
by Willis George Emerson (978-1-63118-423-9)

The Lost Keys of Freemasonry or The Secret of Hiram Abiff
by Manly P. Hall (978-1-63118-427-7)

Rosa Alchemica, The Tables of Law & The Adoration of the Magi
by William Butler Yeats (978-1-63118-421-5)

Ancient Mysteries and Secret Societies by Manly P. Hall
(978-1-63118-410-9)

The Influence of Pythagoras on Freemasonry, the Golden Verses of Pythagoras and the Life and Philosophy of Pythagoras by Albert G. Mackey and Manly P. Hall (978-1-63118-320-1)

The Philosophy of Masonry in Five Parts by Roscoe Pound
(978-1-63118-004-0)

The Story and Legend of Hiram Abiff by William Harvey, Manly P. Hall and Albert G. Mackey
(978-1-63118-411-6)

Audio Versions are also Available on Audible and iTunes

Table of Contents

Introduction...7

Prologue...9

Part I...15

Part II...17

Part III...25

Part IV...39

Introduction

The Apocrypha are a loosely knit series of books, written by early vanguards of Christianity (covering the eras of both the old and new testaments), and which comprise somewhere between about a dozen to several hundred titles, depending on whom you ask and how that person defines "Apocrypha." A small selection of these can still be found included in the Catholic bible, while a majority of the books in question, were abandoned by church officials in the early centuries of Christianity. Many of these apocryphal books were originally considered canon by early followers of Christ, in the first four centuries following his birth. It wasn't until the meeting of the Council of Nicaea in 325, that Emperor Constantine and a group of roughly 300 church bishops, gathered together with the goal of defining, standardizing and unifying an otherwise splintering Christianity, that many of these writings ceased to be included in the newly established canon. Enjoy then, this book as an example, of just one of the many books of the Christian Apocrypha, and be sure to check out other titles in this series.

Prologue

Who is Enoch and why is he so important?

Jude 1:14 describes Enoch as being the seventh generation of man from Adam, while also making reference to Enoch's ability to prophesize. Enoch was born on Seth's side of Adam and Eve's lineage and was the great grandfather of Noah. References to him in the Bible are sparse, but he is most well known for not having died but instead for having walked away with God. In some Christian and Jewish traditions Enoch is also considered to be a scribe and to have been ordained as a priest by Adam.

Perhaps because of Enoch's unique departure from Earth into heaven, there was a rich tradition of exploring what Enoch's life was like, upon leaving Earth. The events of his time in heaven were often explored in classic rabbinical literature as well as the three primary apocryphal books with his name attached to them. Some modern churches continue to embrace Enoch's importance, including the Ethiopian Orthodox Church and perhaps more notably, the Latter Day Saints.

The full text of the magnum opus commonly known as *The Book of Enoch* or *1 Enoch*, is in fact a collection of five separate and unrelated, apocryphal books, the authorship of which spanned several centuries in history, while the real commonality of all being that they each involve Enoch.

The section which is usually presented as chapters 37 through 59 and 61 through 69 of *The Book of Enoch* was originally known as the *Book of Parables* and is actually the most recent of the five collected texts, likely dating between 50 B.C. and 117 A.D. This translation of the *Book of Parables* comes to us from notable scholar of apocryphal literature, R. H. Charles, who published it in 1917.

As always when reading material dealing with Enoch, it's important to remember that much of the text deals with eschatology, or what could be called oracles. Similar to the book entitled *The Vision of Enoch the Righteous*, this book could be considered to be part of a tradition referred to as Apocalyptic Literature, or works that are often denoted by angels delivering prophecies of punishments for the misdeeds of man. The Greek word apocalypse means "revelation" and the numerous works of biblical literature in this category usually involve predictions or visions of the end-times, as revealed by an angel or other heavenly messenger, often told in heavily veiled and colorful symbolism.

The narrative of the *Book of Parables* features two or three distinct characters, the first being Enoch of course, but also an angel identified as "The Son of Man." This angel, "The Son of Man," exhibits characteristics that are reminiscent of the mythical angel Metatron, who was classically considered to be God's personal scribe and often spoke for him. In this regard, Metatron could be described as The Voice of God embodied in an angel. In other words, "The Son of Man" should be viewed as the highest-ranking angel and one who is capable of giving orders to and delivering judgment upon other angels.

At times, the text may seem as if God is speaking in the first person, but it is always the Metatron, or Voice of God who is doing the narrating. And, just as the manager of a business has the ability to speak for the owner and fire employees when needed, the Metatron has been given the authority to speak for God and hand down judgments to sinners.

Later in the text, however, this same title, "The Son of Man", seemingly gets applied to Enoch himself. In these instances, we should keep in mind that in some older, Jewish traditions, the word "Metatron" is the name or title that was given to Enoch, after he walked with God, in heaven. But, it's important not to confuse the title with the individual, since titles are often passed on, from one person to another. As an example, your average church will always have a presiding member of the clergy over the span of one hundred years, but that doesn't mean that it's the same individual for the entire length of time (*in fact, it most certainly isn't*). Titles are fluid and can be transferred or even shared; individuals are specific and unique.

Furthermore, with regards to Enoch, the Metatron and the title of "The Son of Man", it's also important to highlight the fact that not all scholars agree with the above points, as is frequently the case with scholars in any area of study, but even more so when dealing with material as old as this. So, while you are reading these passages, pay close attention to these terms and perhaps more specifically, the context in which they are used, and don't be afraid to make an interpretation for yourself.

Also, in this book you will encounter the terms

"Righteous One" and "Elect One", and within the context of this book, they are fairly interchangeable. These two terms can likely be taken to mean "Messiah" or even "Son of God." However, make sure to pay attention, differentiate and not confuse these terms with the title, "The Son of Man," which we discussed earlier.

Another title you will see in this book is the "Lord of Spirits", and when this occurs, a reference to God himself is being made.

At times it may seem as if there is a hierarchy being suggested that contradicts traditional Christian teachings. After all, the Messiah or Son of God shouldn't be the underling of Enoch or an angel, but that's not what is happening here. These angels understand that there is a hierarchy within their angelic society. As such, the angels in question are simply fulfilling a job assignment given to them by God, and the Messiah knows this, and consequently, he isn't interfering or attempting to micromanage every situation. The Messiah also knows that he has his own duties to fulfill, separate from those of the angels. So, all things are actually working as a well-oiled machine, and not in contradiction with each other, even if it may appear that way on the surface.

The text of the book is broken into three parables, also sometimes called similitudes.

A parable is a story used to illustrate a moral or spiritual lesson. Collectively, these parables given to us by Enoch are done so with the intention of drawing our attention to the watchful eye of God above. Together they focus on a destructive final judgement over a mankind who believes it isn't being watched over anymore and have ceased to behave in a righteous and worthy manner on a daily basis. However, a path of triumph is shown to those who choose to heed it.

In the first parable, the reader is given an announcement of the coming arrival of the Elect One, or Messiah, as well as a prophecy of the harsh judgments which await the sinners of mankind. We see this being contrasted with a future of potential bliss, if mankind chooses a righteous path. There are also glimpses into some of the secrets of heaven.

In the second parable, we see a bit more focus on the Messiah, along with many of the same themes of judgment and prophecy being continued. The division between the sinners and the righteous is also highlighted, as if to remind mankind of the freewill it possesses. We also catch glimpses into the life of Enoch, through conversations and a few descriptions of his ascension into heaven.

In the third and final parable we see further themes of Messianic glory and the angels beginning to make determinations about specific individuals. They fly off to take "measurements" of the righteousness of each man and report back. The angels also begin to reveal the secrets workings of earth, as designed by heaven. We also see several references to Noah and are given a list of the fallen angels.

The book ends with the Messiah firmly seated in his throne, judgements having all been issued and carried out, and the earth has finally been vanquished of sinners with only the righteous remaining.

Book of Parables

Part I

The Announcement from the Son of Man, of the Parables to come

The vision of wisdom, which Enoch the son of Jared, the son of Mahalalel, the son of Cainan, the son of Enos, the son of Seth, the son of Adam, saw…

This is the beginning of the words of wisdom which I lifted up my voice to speak and say to those which dwell on earth: Hear, ye men of old time, and see, ye that come after, the words of the Holy One which I will speak before the Lord of Spirits.

It were better to declare to the men of old time only, but even from those that come after we will not withhold the beginning of wisdom.

Till the present day such wisdom has never been given by the Lord of Spirits as I have received according to my insight, according to the good pleasure of the Lord of Spirits by whom the lot of eternal life has been given to me.

Now three parables were imparted to me, and I lifted up my voice and recounted them to those that dwell on the earth.

Book of Parables

Part II

The First Parable, which includes *"The Coming Judgment of the Wicked"*, *"The Abode of the Righteous and Elect One and the Praises of the Blessed"*, *"The Four Archangels"*, *"The Dwelling-places of Wisdom and of Unrighteousness"* and *"Astronomical Secrets"*

The First Parable, when the congregation of the righteous shall appear, and sinners shall be judged for their sins, and shall be driven from the face of the earth.

And when the Righteous One shall appear before the eyes of the righteous, whose elect works hang upon the Lord of Spirits, and light shall appear to the righteous and the elect who dwell on the earth, where then will be the dwelling of the sinners, and where the resting-place of those who have denied the Lord of Spirits? It would have been good for them if they had not been born.

When the secrets of the righteous shall be revealed and the sinners judged, and the godless driven from the presence of the righteous and elect, from that time those that possess the earth shall no longer be powerful and exalted.

And they shall not be able to behold the face of the holy, for the Lord of Spirits has caused His light to appear on the face of the holy, righteous, and elect.

Then shall the kings and the mighty perish and be given into the hands of the righteous and holy. And thenceforward none shall seek for themselves mercy from the Lord of Spirits, for their life is at an end.

And it shall come to pass in those days that elect and holy children will descend from the high heaven, and their seed will become one with the children of men. And in those days Enoch received books of zeal and wrath, and books of disquiet and expulsion.

And mercy shall not be accorded to them, saith the Lord of Spirits. And in those days a whirlwind carried me off from the earth, and set me down at the end of the heavens.

And there I saw another vision, the dwelling-places of the holy, and the resting-places of the righteous.

Here mine eyes saw their dwellings with His righteous angels, and their resting-places with the holy.

And they petitioned and interceded and prayed for the children of men, and righteousness flowed before them as water, and mercy like dew upon the earth. Thus it is amongst them forever and ever.

And in that place mine eyes saw the Elect One of righteousness and of faith, and I saw his dwelling-place under the wings of the Lord of Spirits.

And righteousness shall prevail in his days, and the righteous and elect shall be without number before Him for ever and ever. And all the righteous and elect before Him shall be strong as fiery lights, and their mouth shall be full of blessing,

And their lips extol the name of the Lord of Spirits, and righteousness before Him shall never fail. There I wished to dwell, and my spirit longed for that dwelling-place.

And there heretofore hath been my portion, for so has it been established concerning me before the Lord of Spirits.

In those days I praised and extolled the name of the Lord of Spirits with blessings and praises, because He hath destined me for blessing and glory according to the good pleasure of the Lord of Spirits. For a long time my eyes regarded that place, and I blessed Him and praised Him, saying:

'Blessed is He, and may He be blessed from the beginning and for evermore. And before Him there is no ceasing. He knows before the world was created what is forever and what will be from generation unto generation. Those who sleep not bless Thee, they stand before Thy glory and bless, praise, and extol, saying, "Holy, holy, holy, is the Lord of Spirits, He filleth the earth with spirits."'

And here my eyes saw all those who sleep not, they stand before Him and bless and say, 'Blessed be Thou, and blessed be the name of the Lord for ever and ever.' And my face was changed, for I could no longer behold.

And after that I saw thousands of thousands and ten thousand times ten thousand, I saw a multitude beyond number and reckoning, who stood before the Lord of Spirits. And on the four sides of the Lord of Spirits I saw four presences, different from those that sleep not, and I learnt their names, for the angel that went with me made known to me their names, and showed me all the hidden things.

And I heard the voices of those four presences as they uttered praises before the Lord of glory. The first voice blesses the Lord of Spirits forever and ever. And the second voice I heard blessing the Elect One and the elect ones who hang upon the Lord of Spirits. And the third voice I heard pray and intercede for those who dwell on the earth and supplicate in the name of the Lord of Spirits. And I heard the fourth voice fending off the Satans and forbidding them to come before the Lord of Spirits to accuse them who dwell on the earth. After that I asked the angel of peace who went with me, who showed me everything that is hidden, 'Who are these four presences which I have seen and whose words I have heard and written down?' And he said to me, 'This first is Michael, the merciful and long-suffering, and the second, who is set over all the diseases and all the wounds of the children of men, is Raphael, and the third, who is set over all the powers, is Gabriel, and the fourth, who is set over the repentance unto hope of those who inherit eternal life, is named Phanuel.' And these are the four angels of the Lord of Spirits and the four voices I heard in those days.

Wisdom found no place where she might dwell, then a

dwelling-place was assigned her in the heavens. Wisdom went forth to make her dwelling among the children of men, and found no dwelling-place. Wisdom returned to her place, and took her seat among the angels.

And unrighteousness went forth from her chambers, whom she sought not she found, and dwelt with them, as rain in a desert and dew on a thirsty land.

And after that I saw all the secrets of the heavens, and how the kingdom is divided, and how the actions of men are weighed in the balance. And there I saw the mansions of the elect and the mansions of the holy, and mine eyes saw there all the sinners being driven from thence which deny the name of the Lord of Spirits, and being dragged off, and they could not abide because of the punishment which proceeds from the Lord of Spirits.

And there mine eyes saw the secrets of the lightning and of the thunder, and the secrets of the winds, how they are divided to blow over the earth, and the secrets of the clouds and dew, and there I saw from whence they proceed in that place and from whence they saturate the dusty earth. And there I saw closed chambers out of which the winds are divided, the chamber of the hail and winds, the chamber of the mist, and of the clouds, and the cloud thereof hovers over the earth from the beginning of the world. And I saw the chambers of the sun and moon, whence they proceed and whither they come again, and their glorious return, and how one is superior to the other, and their stately orbit, and how they do not leave their orbit, and they add nothing to their orbit and they take nothing from it, and they keep faith with each other, in accordance with the oath by which they are bound together. And first the sun goes forth and traverses his path according to the commandment of the Lord of Spirits, and mighty is His name forever and ever.

And after that I saw the hidden and the visible path of the moon, and she accomplishes the course of her path in that place by day and by night--the one holding a position opposite to the other before the Lord of Spirits.

And they give thanks and praise and rest not, for unto them is their thanksgiving rest. For the sun changes oft for a blessing or a curse, and the course of the path of the moon is light to the righteous and darkness to the sinners in the name of the Lord, who made a separation between the light and the darkness, and divided the spirits of men, and strengthened the spirits of the righteous, in the name of His righteousness.

For no angel hinders and no power is able to hinder, for He appoints a judge for them all and He judges them all before Him.

And I saw other lightnings and the stars of heaven, and I saw how He called them all by their names and they hearkened unto Him. And I saw how they are weighed in a righteous balance according to their proportions of light. I saw the width of their spaces and the day of their appearing, and how their revolution produces lightning, and I saw their revolution according to the number of the angels, and how they keep faith with each other. And I asked the angel who went with me who showed me what was hidden, 'What are these?' And he said to me, 'The Lord of Spirits hath showed thee their parabolic meaning, these are the names of the holy who dwell on the earth and believe in the name of the Lord of Spirits for ever and ever.'

Book of Parables

Part III

The Second Parable, which includes *"The Lot of the Apostates: the New Heaven and the New Earth"*, *"The Head of Days and the Son of Man"*, *"The Prayer of the Righteous for Vengeance and their Joy at its Coming"*, *"The Fount of Righteousness; the Son of Man-- the Stay of the Righteous: Judgement of the Kings and the Mighty"*, *"The Power and Wisdom of the Elect One"*, *"The Glorification and Victory of the Righteous: the Repentance of the Gentiles"*, *"The Resurrection of the Dead, and the Separation by the Judge of the Righteous and the Wicked"*, *"The Seven Metal Mountains and the Elect One"*, *"The Valley of Judgement: the Angels of Punishment: the Communities of the Elect One"*, and *"The Return from the Dispersion"*

And this is the Second Parable concerning those who deny the name of the dwelling of the holy ones and the Lord of Spirits.

And into the heaven they shall not ascend, And on the earth they shall not come: Such shall be the lot of the sinners Who have denied the name of the Lord of Spirits, Who are thus preserved for the day of suffering and tribulation.

On that day Mine Elect One shall sit on the throne of glory And shall try their works, And their places of rest shall be innumerable.

And their souls shall grow strong within them when they see Mine Elect Ones, And those who have called upon My glorious name:

Then will I cause Mine Elect One to dwell among them.

And I will transform the heaven and make it an eternal blessing and light

And I will transform the earth and make it a blessing:

And I will cause Mine Elect Ones to dwell upon it: But the sinners and evil-doers shall not set foot thereon.

For I have provided and satisfied with peace My righteous ones And have caused them to dwell before Me:

But for the sinners there is judgement impending with Me, So that I shall destroy them from the face of the earth.

And there I saw One who had a Head of Days, And His head was white like wool, And with Him was another being whose countenance had the appearance of a man, And his face was full of graciousness, like one of the holy angels.

And I asked the angel who went with me and showed me all the hidden things, concerning that Son of Man, who he was, and whence he was, and why he went with the Head of Days? And he answered and said unto me:

This is the Son of Man who hath righteousness, With

whom dwelleth righteousness, And who revealeth all the treasures of that which is hidden,

Because the Lord of Spirits hath chosen him, And whose lot hath the pre-eminence before the Lord of Spirits in uprightness forever.

And this Son of Man whom thou hast seen Shall raise up the kings and the mighty from their seats, And the strong from their thrones

And shall loosen the reins of the strong, And break the teeth of the sinners.

And he shall put down the kings from their thrones and kingdoms Because they do not extol and praise Him, Nor humbly acknowledge whence the kingdom was bestowed upon them.

And he shall put down the countenance of the strong, And shall fill them with shame.

And darkness shall be their dwelling, And worms shall be their bed, And they shall have no hope of rising from their beds, Because they do not extol the name of the Lord of Spirits.

And these are they who judge the stars of heaven, And raise their hands against the Most High, And tread upon the earth and dwell upon it.

And all their deeds manifest unrighteousness, And their

power rests upon their riches, And their faith is in the gods which they have made with their hands, And they deny the name of the Lord of Spirits,

And they persecute the houses of His congregations, And the faithful who hang upon the name of the Lord of Spirits.

And in those days shall have ascended the prayer of the righteous, And the blood of the righteous from the earth before the Lord of Spirits.

In those days the holy ones who dwell above in the heavens Shall unite with one voice And supplicate and pray and praise, And give thanks and bless the name of the Lord of Spirits, On behalf of the blood of the righteous which has been shed,

And that the prayer of the righteous may not be in vain before the Lord of Spirits, That judgement may be done unto them, And that they may not have to suffer forever.

In those days I saw the Head of Days when He seated himself upon the throne of His glory, And the books of the living were opened before Him: And all His host which is in heaven above and His counselors stood before Him,

And the hearts of the holy were filled with joy; Because the number of the righteous had been offered, And the prayer of the righteous had been heard, And the blood of the righteous been required before the Lord of Spirits.

And in that place I saw the fountain of righteousness

Which was inexhaustible: And around it were many fountains of wisdom;

And all the thirsty drank of them, And were filled with wisdom, And their dwellings were with the righteous and holy and elect.

And at that hour that Son of Man was named In the presence of the Lord of Spirits, And his name before the Head of Days.

Yea, before the sun and the signs were created, Before the stars of the heaven were made, His name was named before the Lord of Spirits.

He shall be a staff to the righteous whereon to stay themselves and not fall, And he shall be the light of the Gentiles, And the hope of those who are troubled of heart.

All who dwell on earth shall fall down and worship before him, And will praise and bless and celebrate with song the Lord of Spirits.

And for this reason hath he been chosen and hidden before Him, Before the creation of the world and for evermore.

And the wisdom of the Lord of Spirits hath revealed him to the holy and righteous; For he hath preserved the lot of the righteous, Because they have hated and despised this world of unrighteousness, And have hated all its works and ways in the name of the Lord of Spirits: For in his name they are saved,

And according to his good pleasure hath it been in regard to their life.

In these days downcast in countenance shall the kings of the earth have become, And the strong who possess the land because of the works of their hands;

For on the day of their anguish and affliction they shall not be able to save themselves.

And I will give them over into the hands of Mine elect:

As straw in the fire so shall they burn before the face of the holy: As lead in the water shall they sink before the face of the righteous, And no trace of them shall any more be found.

And on the day of their affliction there shall be rest on the earth, And before them they shall fall and not rise again:

And there shall be no one to take them with his hands and raise them: For they have denied the Lord of Spirits and His Anointed. The name of the Lord of Spirits be blessed.

For wisdom is poured out like water, And glory faileth not before him for evermore.

For he is mighty in all the secrets of righteousness, And unrighteousness shall disappear as a shadow, And have no continuance; Because the Elect One standeth before the Lord of Spirits, And his glory is for ever and ever, And his might unto all generations.

And in him dwells the spirit of wisdom, And the spirit which gives insight, And the spirit of understanding and of might, And the spirit of those who have fallen asleep in righteousness.

And he shall judge the secret things, And none shall be able to utter a lying word before him; For he is the Elect One before the Lord of Spirits according to His good pleasure.

And in those days a change shall take place for the holy and elect, And the light of days shall abide upon them, And glory and honor shall turn to the holy,

On the day of affliction on which evil shall have been treasured up against the sinners.

And the righteous shall be victorious in the name of the Lord of Spirits: And He will cause the others to witness this That they may repent And forgo the works of their hands.

They shall have no honor through the name of the Lord of Spirits, Yet through His name shall they be saved, And the Lord of Spirits will have compassion on them, For His compassion is great.

And He is righteous also in His judgement, And in the presence of His glory unrighteousness also shall not maintain itself: At His judgement the unrepentant shall perish before Him.

And from henceforth I will have no mercy on them, saith

the Lord of Spirits.

And in those days shall the earth also give back that which has been entrusted to it, And Sheol also shall give back that which it has received, And hell shall give back that which it owes.

For in those days the Elect One shall arise,

And he shall choose the righteous and holy from among them: For the day has drawn nigh that they should be saved.

And the Elect One shall in those days sit on My throne, And his mouth shall pour forth all the secrets of wisdom and counsel: For the Lord of Spirits hath given them to him and hath glorified him.

And in those days shall the mountains leap like rams, And the hills also shall skip like lambs satisfied with milk, And the faces of all the angels in heaven shall be lighted up with joy.

And the earth shall rejoice,

And the righteous shall dwell upon it,

And the elect shall walk thereon.

And after those days in that place where I had seen all the visions of that which is hidden--for I had been carried off in a whirlwind and they had borne me towards the west—

There mine eyes saw all the secret things of heaven that shall be, a mountain of iron, and a mountain of copper, and a mountain of silver, and a mountain of gold, and a mountain of soft metal, and a mountain of lead.

And I asked the angel who went with me, saying, 'What things are these which I have seen in secret?'

And he said unto me: 'All these things which thou hast seen shall serve the dominion of His Anointed that he may be potent and mighty on the earth.'

And that angel of peace answered, saying unto me: 'Wait a little, and there shall be revealed unto thee all the secret things which surround the Lord of Spirits.

And these mountains which thine eyes have seen, The mountain of iron, and the mountain of copper, and the mountain of silver, And the mountain of gold, and the mountain of soft metal, and the mountain of lead, All these shall be in the presence of the Elect One As wax: before the fire, And like the water which streams down from above upon those mountains, And they shall become powerless before his feet.

And it shall come to pass in those days that none shall be saved, Either by gold or by silver, And none be able to escape.

And there shall be no iron for war, Nor shall one clothe oneself with a breastplate. Bronze shall be of no service, And tin shall be of no service and shall not be esteemed, And lead shall not be desired.

And all these things shall be denied and destroyed from the surface of the earth, When the Elect One shall appear before the face of the Lord of Spirits.

There mine eyes saw a deep valley with open mouths, and all who dwell on the earth and sea and islands shall bring to him gifts and presents and tokens of homage, but that deep valley shall not become full.

And their hands commit lawless deeds, And the sinners devour all whom they lawlessly oppress: Yet the sinners shall be destroyed before the face of the Lord of Spirits, And they shall be banished from off the face of His earth, And they shall perish for ever and ever.

For I saw all the angels of punishment abiding there and preparing all the instruments of Satan.

And I asked the angel of peace who went with me: For whom are they preparing these instruments?

And he said unto me: They prepare these for the kings and the mighty of this earth, that they may thereby be destroyed.

And after this the Righteous and Elect One shall cause the house of his congregation to appear: henceforth they shall be no more hindered in the name of the Lord of Spirits.

And these mountains shall not stand as the earth before his

righteousness, But the hills shall be as a fountain of water, And the righteous shall have rest from the oppression of sinners.

And I looked and turned to another part of the earth, and saw there a deep valley with burning fire.

And they brought the kings and the mighty, and began to cast them into this deep valley.

And there mine eyes saw how they made these their instruments, iron chains of immeasurable weight.

And I asked the angel of peace who went with me, saying: For whom are these chains being prepared?

And he said unto me: These are being prepared for the hosts of Azazel, so that they may take them and cast them into the abyss of complete condemnation, and they shall cover their jaws with rough stones as the Lord of Spirits commanded.

And Michael, and Gabriel, and Raphael, and Phanuel shall take hold of them on that great day, and cast them on that day into the burning furnace, that the Lord of Spirits may take vengeance on them for their unrighteousness in becoming subject to Satan and leading astray those who dwell on the earth.

When I have desired to take hold of them by the hand of the angels on the day of tribulation and pain because of this, I will cause My chastisement and My wrath to abide upon them, saith God, the Lord of Spirits.

Ye mighty kings who dwell on the earth, ye shall have to behold Mine Elect One, how he sits on the throne of glory and judges Azazel, and all his associates, and all his hosts in the name of the Lord of Spirits.

And I saw there the hosts of the angels of punishment going, and they held scourges and chains of iron and bronze.

And I asked the angel of peace who went with me, saying: To whom are these who hold the scourges going?

And he said unto me: To their elect and beloved ones, that they may be cast into the chasm of the abyss of the valley.

And then that valley shall be filled with their elect and beloved, And the days of their lives shall be at an end, And the days of their leading astray shall not thenceforward be reckoned.

And in those days the angels shall return And hurl themselves to the east upon the Parthians and Medes: They shall stir up the kings, so that a spirit of unrest shall come upon them, And they shall rouse them from their thrones, That they may break forth as lions from their lairs, And as hungry wolves among their flocks.

And they shall go up and tread underfoot the land of His elect ones, And the land of His elect ones shall be before them a threshing-floor and a highway:

But the city of my righteous shall be a hindrance to their

horses.

And they shall begin to fight among themselves, And their right hand shall be strong against themselves,

And a man shall not know his brother, Nor a son his father or his mother,

Till there be no number of the corpses through their slaughter, And their punishment be not in vain.

In those days Sheol shall open its jaws, And they shall be swallowed up therein

And their destruction shall be at an end; Sheol shall devour the sinners in the presence of the elect.

And it came to pass after this that I saw another host of wagons, and men riding thereon, and coming on the winds from the east, and from the west to the south.

And the noise of their wagons was heard, and when this turmoil took place the holy ones from heaven remarked it, and the pillars of the earth were moved from their place, and the sound thereof was heard from the one end of heaven to the other, in one day.

And they shall all fall down and worship the Lord of Spirits.

And this is the end of the second Parable.

Book of Parables

Part IV

The Third Parable, including *"The Blessedness of the Saints"*, *"The Lights and the Thunder"*, *"Angels go off to Measure Paradise: the Judgement of the Righteous by the Elect One: the Praise of the Elect One and of God"*, *"Judgement of the Kings and the Mighty: Blessedness of the Righteous"*, *"The Unavailing Repentance of the Kings and the Mighty"*, *"Vision of the Fallen Angels in the Place of Punishment"*, *"Enoch Foretells to Noah the Deluge and his own Preservation"*, *"God's Promise to Noah: Places of Punishment of the Angels and of the Kings"*, *"Michael and Raphael Astonished at the Severity of the Judgement"*, *"The Names and Functions of the Fallen Angels and Satan's Secret Oath"* and *"Close of the Third Parable"*

And I began to speak the third Parable concerning the righteous and elect.

Blessed are ye, ye righteous and elect, For glorious shall be your lot.

And the righteous shall be in the light of the sun. And the elect in the light of eternal life: The days of their life shall be unending, And the days of the holy without number.

And they shall seek the light and find righteousness with the Lord of Spirits: There shall be peace to the righteous in the name of the Eternal Lord.

And after this it shall be said to the holy in heaven That they should seek out the secrets of righteousness, the heritage of faith: For it has become bright as the sun upon earth, And the darkness is past.

And there shall be a light that never endeth, And to a limit of days they shall not come, For the darkness shall first have been destroyed, And the light established before the Lord of Spirits, And the light of uprightness established for ever before the Lord of Spirits.

In those days mine eyes saw the secrets of the lightnings, and of the lights, and the judgements they execute: and they lighten for a blessing or a curse as the Lord of Spirits willeth.

And there I saw the secrets of the thunder, and how when it resounds above in the heaven, the sound thereof is heard, and he caused me to see the judgements executed on the earth, whether they be for well-being and blessing, or for a curse according to the word of the Lord of Spirits.

And after that all the secrets of the lights and lightnings were shown to me, and they lighten for blessing and for satisfying.

And I saw in those days how long cords were given to those angels, and they took to themselves wings and flew, and they went towards the north.

And I asked the angel, saying unto him: Why have those angels taken these cords and gone off? And he said unto me:

They have gone to measure.

And the angel who went with me said unto me: These shall bring the measures of the righteous, And the ropes of the righteous to the righteous, That they may stay themselves on the name of the Lord of Spirits for ever and ever.

The elect shall begin to dwell with the elect, And those are the measures which shall be given to faith And which shall strengthen righteousness.

And these measures shall also reveal all the secrets of the depths of the earth, And those who have been destroyed by the desert, And those who have been devoured by the beasts, And those who have been devoured by the fish of the sea,

That they may return and stay themselves On the day of the Elect One; For none shall be destroyed before the Lord of Spirits, And none can be destroyed.

And all who dwell above in the heaven received a command and power and one voice and one light like unto fire.

And that One with their first words they blessed, And extolled and lauded with wisdom, And they were wise in utterance and in the spirit of life.

And the Lord of Spirits placed the Elect one on the throne of glory. And he shall judge all the works of the holy above in the heaven, And in the balance shall their deeds be weighed

And when he shall lift up his countenance To judge their secret ways according to the word of the name of the Lord of Spirits, And their path according to the way of the righteous judgement of the Lord of Spirits, Then shall they all with one voice speak and bless, And glorify and extol and sanctify the name of the Lord of Spirits.

And He will summon all the host of the heavens, and all the holy ones above, and the host of God, the Cherubic, Seraphin and Ophannin, and all the angels of power, and all the angels of principalities, and the Elect One, and the other powers on the earth and over the water.

On that day shall raise one voice, and bless and glorify and exalt in the spirit of faith, and in the spirit of wisdom, and in the spirit of patience, and in the spirit of mercy, and in the spirit of judgement and of peace, and in the spirit of goodness, and shall all say with one voice: Blessed is He, and may the name of the Lord of Spirits be blessed for ever and ever.

All who sleep not above in heaven shall bless Him: All the holy ones who are in heaven shall bless Him, And all the elect who dwell in the garden of life:

And every spirit of light who is able to bless, and glorify, and extol, and hallow Thy blessed name, And all flesh shall beyond measure glorify and bless Thy name for ever and ever.

For great is the mercy of the Lord of Spirits, and He is long-suffering, And all His works and all that He has created He has revealed to the righteous and elect In the name of the Lord of

Spirits.

And thus the Lord commanded the kings and the mighty and the exalted, and those who dwell on the earth, and said: Open your eyes and lift up your horns if ye are able to recognize the Elect One.

And the Lord of Spirits seated him on the throne of His glory, And the spirit of righteousness was poured out upon him, And the word of his mouth slays all the sinners, And all the unrighteous are destroyed from before his face.

And there shall stand up in that day all the kings and the mighty, And the exalted and those who hold the earth, And they shall see and recognize How he sits on the throne of his glory, And righteousness is judged before him, And no lying word is spoken before him.

Then shall pain come upon them as on a woman in travail, And she has pain in bringing forth, When her child enters the mouth of the womb, And she has pain in bringing forth.

And one portion of them shall look on the other, And they shall be terrified, And they shall be downcast of countenance, And pain shall seize them, When they see that Son of Man Sitting on the throne of his glory.

And the kings and the mighty and all who possess the earth shall bless and glorify and extol him who rules over all, who was hidden.

For from the beginning the Son of Man was hidden, And the Most High preserved him in the presence of His might, And revealed him to the elect.

And the congregation of the elect and holy shall be sown, And all the elect shall stand before him on that day.

And all the kings and the mighty and the exalted and those who rule the earth Shall fall down before him on their faces, And worship and set their hope upon that Son of Man, And petition him and supplicate for mercy at his hands.

Nevertheless that Lord of Spirits will so press them That they shall hastily go forth from His presence, And their faces shall be filled with shame, And the darkness grow deeper on their faces.

And He will deliver them to the angels for punishment, To execute vengeance on them because they have oppressed His children and His elect

And they shall be a spectacle for the righteous and for His elect: They shall rejoice over them, Because the wrath of the Lord of Spirits resteth upon them, And His sword is drunk with their blood.

And the righteous and elect shall be saved on that day, And they shall never thenceforward see the face of the sinners and unrighteous.

And the Lord of Spirits will abide over them, And with that

Son of Man shall they eat And lie down and rise up for ever and ever.

And the righteous and elect shall have risen from the earth, And ceased to be of downcast countenance.

And they shall have been clothed with garments of glory,

And these shall be the garments of life from the Lord of Spirits: And your garments shall not grow old, Nor your glory pass away before the Lord of Spirits.

In those days shall the mighty and the kings who possess the earth implore Him to grant them a little respite from His angels of punishment to whom they were delivered, that they might fall down and worship before the Lord of Spirits, and confess their sins before Him.

And they shall bless and glorify the Lord of Spirits, and say:

Blessed is the Lord of Spirits and the Lord of kings, And the Lord of the mighty and the Lord of the rich, And the Lord of glory and the Lord of wisdom,

And splendid in every secret thing is Thy power from generation to generation, And Thy glory for ever and ever:

Deep are all Thy secrets and innumerable, And Thy righteousness is beyond reckoning.

We have now learnt that we should glorify And bless the

Lord of kings and Him who is king over all kings.

And they shall say: Would that we had rest to glorify and give thanks And confess our faith before His glory!

And now we long for a little rest but find it not: We follow hard upon and obtain it not:

And light has vanished from before us, And darkness is our dwelling-place for ever and ever:

For we have not believed before Him Nor glorified the name of the Lord of Spirits, nor glorified our Lord

But our hope was in the scepter of our kingdom, And in our glory.

And in the day of our suffering and tribulation He saves us not, And we find no respite for confession

That our Lord is true in all His works, and in His judgements and His justice, And His judgements have no respect of persons.

And we pass away from before His face on account of our works, And all our sins are reckoned up in righteousness.

Now they shall say unto themselves: Our souls are full of unrighteous gain, but it does not prevent us from descending from the midst thereof into the burden of Sheol.

And after that their faces shall be filled with darkness And shame before that Son of Man, And they shall be driven from his presence, And the sword shall abide before his face in their midst.

Thus spoke the Lord of Spirits: This is the ordinance and judgement with respect to the mighty and the kings and the exalted and those who possess the earth before the Lord of Spirits.

And other forms I saw hidden in that place.

I heard the voice of the angel saying: These are the angels who descended to the earth, and revealed what was hidden to the children of men and seduced the children of men into committing sin.

And in those days Noah saw the earth that it had sunk down and its destruction was nigh.

And he arose from thence and went to the ends of the earth, and cried aloud to his grandfather Enoch: and Noah said three times with an embittered voice: Hear me, hear me, hear me.

And I said unto him: Tell me what it is that is falling out on the earth that the earth is in such evil plight and shaken, lest perchance I shall perish with it?

And thereupon there was a great commotion, on the earth, and a voice was heard from heaven, and I fell on my face.

And Enoch my grandfather came and stood by me, and said unto me: Why hast thou cried unto me with a bitter cry and weeping?

And a command has gone forth from the presence of the Lord concerning those who dwell on the earth that their ruin is accomplished because they have learnt all the secrets of the angels, and all the violence of the Satans, and all their powers--the most secret ones--and all the power of those who practice sorcery, and the power of witchcraft, and the power of those who make molten images for the whole earth:

And how silver is produced from the dust of the earth, and how soft metal originates in the earth.

For lead and tin are not produced from the earth like the first: it is a fountain that produces them, and an angel stands therein, and that angel is pre-eminent.

And after that my grandfather Enoch took hold of me by my hand and raised me up, and said unto me: Go, for I have asked the Lord of Spirits as touching this commotion on the earth.

And He said unto me: Because of their unrighteousness their judgement has been determined upon and shall not be withheld by Me forever. Because of the sorceries which they have searched out and learnt, the earth and those who dwell upon it shall be destroyed.

And these--they have no place of repentance forever,

because they have shown them what was hidden, and they are the damned: but as for thee, my son, the Lord of Spirits knows that thou art pure, and guiltless of this reproach concerning the secrets.

And He has destined thy name to be among the holy, And will preserve thee amongst those who dwell on the earth, And has destined thy righteous seed both for kingship and for great honors, And from thy seed shall proceed a fountain of the righteous and holy without number forever.

And after that he showed me the angels of punishment who are prepared to come and let loose all the powers of the waters which are beneath in the earth in order to bring judgement and destruction on all who abide and dwell on the earth.

And the Lord of Spirits gave commandment to the angels who were going forth, that they should not cause the waters to rise but should hold them in check; for those angels were over the powers of the waters.

And I went away from the presence of Enoch.

And in those days the word of God came unto me, and He said unto me: Noah, thy lot has come up before Me, a lot without blame, a lot of love and uprightness.

And now the angels are making a wooden building, and when they have completed that task I will place My hand upon it and preserve it, and there shall come forth from it the seed of life, and a change shall set in so that the earth will not remain without inhabitant.

And I will make fast thy seed before me for ever and ever, and I will spread abroad those who dwell with thee: it shall not be unfruitful on the face of the earth, but it shall be blessed and multiply on the earth in the name of the Lord.

And He will imprison those angels, who have shown unrighteousness, in that burning valley which my grandfather Enoch had formerly shown to me in the west among the mountains of gold and silver and iron and soft metal and tin.

And I saw that valley in which there was a great convulsion and a convulsion of the waters.

And when all this took place, from that fiery molten metal and from the convulsion thereof in that place, there was produced a smell of sulfur, and it was connected with those waters, and that valley of the angels who had led astray mankind burned beneath that land.

And through its valleys proceed streams of fire, where these angels are punished who had led astray those who dwell upon the earth.

But those waters shall in those days serve for the kings and the mighty and the exalted, and those who dwell on the earth, for the healing of the body, but for the punishment of the spirit; now their spirit is full of lust, that they may be punished in their body, for they have denied the Lord of Spirits and see their punishment daily, and yet believe not in His name.

And in proportion as the burning of their bodies becomes severe, a corresponding change shall take place in their spirit for ever and ever; for before the Lord of Spirits none shall utter an idle word.

For the judgement shall come upon them, because they believe in the lust of their body and deny the Spirit of the Lord.

And those same waters will undergo a change in those days; for when those angels are punished in these waters, these water-springs shall change their temperature, and when the angels ascend, this water of the springs shall change and become cold.

And I heard Michael answering and saying: This judgement wherewith the angels are judged is a testimony for the kings and the mighty who possess the earth.

Because these waters of judgement minister to the healing of the body of the kings and the lust of their body; therefore, they will not see and will not believe that those waters will change and become a fire which burns forever.

And after Enoch gave the teaching of all the secrets in the book in the Parables which had been given to him, and he put them together for me in the words of the *Book of the Parables*.

And on that day Michael answered Raphael and said: The power of the spirit transports and makes me to tremble because of the severity of the judgement of the secrets, the judgement of the angels: who can endure the severe judgement which has been executed, and before which they melt away?

And Michael answered again, and said to Raphael: Who is he whose heart is not softened concerning it, and whose reins are not troubled by this word of judgement that has gone forth upon them because of those who have thus led them out?

And it came to pass when he stood before the Lord of Spirits, Michael said thus to Raphael: I will not take their part under the eye of the Lord; for the Lord of Spirits has been angry with them because they do as if they were the Lord. Therefore, all that is hidden shall come upon them for ever and ever; for neither angel nor man shall have his portion in it, but alone they have received their judgement for ever and ever.

And after this judgement they shall terrify and make them to tremble because they have shown this to those who dwell on the earth.

And behold the names of those angels and these are their names: the first of them is Samjaza, the second Artaqifa, and the third Armen, the fourth Kokabel, the fifth Turael, the sixth Rumjal, the seventh Danjal, the eighth Neqael, the ninth Baraqel, the tenth Azazel, the eleventh Armaros, the twelfth Batarjal, the thirteenth Busasejal, the fourteenth Hananel, the fifteenth Turel, and the sixteenth Simapesiel, the seventeenth Jetrel, the eighteenth Tumael, the nineteenth Turel, the twentieth Rumael, the twenty-first Azazel.

And these are the chiefs of their angels and their names,

and their chief ones over hundreds and over fifties and over tens.

The name of the first Jeqon: that is, the one who led astray all the sons of God, and brought them down to the earth, and led them astray through the daughters of men.

And the second was named Asbeel: he imparted to the holy sons of God evil counsel, and led them astray so that they defiled their bodies with the daughters of men.

And the third was named Gadreel: he it is who showed the children of men all the blows of death, and he led astray Eve, and showed the weapons of death to the sons of men the shield and the coat of mail, and the sword for battle, and all the weapons of death to the children of men.

And from his hand they have proceeded against those who dwell on the earth from that day and for evermore.

And the fourth was named Penemue: he taught the children of men the bitter and the sweet, and he taught them all the secrets of their wisdom.

And he instructed mankind in writing with ink and paper, and thereby many sinned from eternity to eternity and until this day.

For men were not created for such a purpose, to give confirmation to their good faith with pen and ink.

For men were created exactly like the angels, to the intent that they should continue pure and righteous, and death, which destroys everything, could not have taken hold of them, but through this their knowledge they are perishing, and through this power it is consuming me.

And the fifth was named Kasdeja: this is he who showed the children of men all the wicked smitings of spirits and demons, and the smitings of the embryo in the womb, that it may pass away, and the smitings of the soul the bites of the serpent, and the smitings which befall through the noontide heat, the son of the serpent named Tabaa'et.

And this is the task of Kasbeel, the chief of the oath which he showed to the holy ones when he dwelt high above in glory, and its name is Biqa.

This angel requested Michael to show him the hidden name, that he might enunciate it in the oath, so that those might quake before that name and oath who revealed all that was in secret to the children of men.

And this is the power of this oath, for it is powerful and strong, and he placed this oath Akae in the hand of Michael.

And these are the secrets of this oath . . .

And they are strong through his oath: And the heaven was suspended before the world was created, And forever.

And through it the earth was founded upon the water, And

from the secret recesses of the mountains come beautiful waters, From the creation of the world and unto eternity.

And through that oath the sea was created, And as its foundation He set for it the sand against the time of its anger, And it dare not pass beyond it from the creation of the world unto eternity.

And through that oath are the depths made fast, And abide and stir not from their place from eternity to eternity.

And through that oath the sun and moon complete their course, And deviate not from their ordinance from eternity to eternity.

And through that oath the stars complete their course, And He calls them by their names, And they answer Him from eternity to eternity.

And in like manner the spirits of the water, and of the winds, and of all zephyrs, and their paths from all the quarters of the winds.

And there are preserved the voices of the thunder and the light of the lightnings: and there are preserved the chambers of the hail and the chambers of the hoarfrost, and the chambers of the mist, and the chambers of the rain and the dew.

And all these believe and give thanks before the Lord of Spirits, and glorify Him with all their power, and their food is in every act of thanksgiving: they thank and glorify and extol the name of the Lord of Spirits for ever and ever.

And this oath is mighty over them And through it they are preserved and their paths are preserved, And their course is not destroyed.

And there was great joy amongst them, And they blessed and glorified and extolled Because the name of that Son of Man had been revealed unto them.

And he sat on the throne of his glory, And the sum of judgement was given unto the Son of Man, And he caused the sinners to pass away and be destroyed from off the face of the earth, And those who have led the world astray.

With chains shall they be bound, And in their assemblage-place of destruction shall they be imprisoned, And all their works vanish from the face of the earth.

And from henceforth there shall be nothing corruptible; For that Son of Man has appeared, And has seated himself on the throne of his glory, And all evil shall pass away before his face, And the word of that Son of Man shall go forth And be strong before the Lord of Spirits.

Thus is the end of the Parables of Enoch.

www.ingramcontent.com/pod-product-compliance
Lightning Source LLC
LaVergne TN
LVHW041500070426
835507LV00009B/711